TECH GIRLS™

Careers for

TECH GIRLS IN ENGINEERING

MARCIA AMIDON LUSTED

ROSEN
PUBLISHING®

New York

Published in 2016 by The Rosen Publishing Group, Inc.
29 East 21st Street, New York, NY 10010

Library of Congress Cataloging-in-Publication Data

Lusted, Marcia Amidon.
Careers for tech girls in engineering/Marcia Amidon Lusted.—First edition.
    pages cm.—(Tech girls)
Includes bibliographical references and index.
ISBN 978-1-4994-6097-1 (library bound)
1. Engineering—Vocational guidance—Juvenile literature. 2. Women in engineering—Juvenile literature. I. Title.
TA157.5.L87 2016
620.0023—dc23

                                                                          2014045155

Manufactured in the United States of America

CONTENTS

Introduction

A group of high school students moves through a plant that manufactures ball bearings for the aerospace industry (and also has an internship program for potential engineering students). These students are part of the pre-engineering class at their school, and today is National Manufacturer's Day. It's a chance for students to see what really goes on inside a workplace that relies heavily on engineering. But another goal behind the tour is to show the girls in the group—who are outnumbered by boys—that women have as many opportunities in engineering as men do. The number of women who go to college for engineering is smaller than it was in the 1970s, and yet the need for good engineers is more important than ever before. According to the U.S. Bureau of Labor Statistics, the engineering profession is expected to grow by 20 percent over the next ten years. That's a faster average growth rate than for all other occupations. In fact, any STEM (science, technology, engineering, and mathematics) career is in high demand and vitally important to the workforce right now. However, many girls who are really good at science, math, and technology don't consider going into engineering. Some just need a push, or a little help to see what kinds of opportunities there are and how it might be a good fit for their skills.

Stacey DelVecchio, who is an engineer for Caterpillar, Inc., where she works in product development, remembers getting that push herself:

[I was] a little lost as to what I wanted to be when I grew up, a question we often ask kids, especially as they get into high school. I just didn't know. All I knew was what I didn't want to do. I did however love to learn and really enjoyed numbers. I used to count everything and could do math in my head at the drop of the hat. I also thought science was pretty cool. This is where my parents really helped out. They thought engineering might be a good career for me and had me talk to family friends and relatives. While I'm not sure these conversations created a burning desire for me to be an engineer, I do think they kept my curiosity piqued.

Stacey feels that the encouragement to study chemical engineering was what brought her not only to a successful career but also to have "the opportunity to change the world as an engineer."

The girls who participated in the manufacturing tour were just as engaged and interested as the guys, and the teachers who accompanied the group admitted that many of the girls were better students as well. So if a girl is good at math and loves science and thinks technology and problem-solving are exciting,

Many industries desperately need qualified engineers, and women are great candidates to fill these roles.

why should she stand back and let the guys have all the fun? Girls with these skills and abilities are sorely needed as the demand for engineers goes up and there aren't enough qualified people to fill those jobs. And to get there, they will need a strong STEM education, including real-world opportunities with engineers.

Intrigued? Then it's time to get started. This resource provides tools and resources needed to prepare for a career in engineering. From just what an engineer is, to the necessary classes, to the activities and other programs that will strengthen classroom knowledge, tech girls will find what they need to achieve a cool career…and perhaps, like Stacey DelVecchio, change the world through engineering.

Chapter one

ENGINEERS...THEY DON'T DRIVE TRAINS

What does the word *engineer* bring to mind when it comes to careers? You might think engineers are those people who drive huge locomotives pulling strings of freight cars. While that's a perfectly great career, the kind of engineer that's of interest to tech-savvy girls is completely different.

ENDLESS POSSIBILITIES

By definition, an engineer is someone who designs, builds, and maintains machinery, engines, or public works. But that's a pretty narrow description of all the things that engineers do in today's world. The National Action Council for Minorities in Engineering describes many different types of engineers on its website. Engineers might be involved in the aerospace industry, designing airplanes and space vehicles. Agricultural and biological engineers work with crops, such as creating disease-resistant or higher producing food sources, or work to protect the environment and use natural resources well. Bioengineering and biochemical engineers also work with the environment, specifically, studying living systems and applying that knowledge to solving other problems, such as destroying waste and cleaning up contamination. Audio engineers work with sound systems, recording, and other sound-related projects. Biomedical engineers study biology and medicine to improve health care. Ceramics and materials engineers, as well as chemical engineers, work with different kinds of materials to provide new technology for inventors or improve existing materials. Civil engineers work in construction of structures such as skyscrapers and tunnels, translating an architect's ideas into reality or repairing existing public works. There are also computer and electrical engineers, as well as geological, industrial, marine, environmental, mining, mechanical, nuclear, and petroleum engineers.

Engineers work in many different industries, including designing, building, and programming robots.

The list is nearly endless, so no matter what piques your curiosity, there is probably an engineering career to go with it.

On the Engineering Your Future website, sponsored by the Engineering and Science Foundation, it asks: "Can you see yourself: Building robots? Managing the production of a new wonder drug? Developing a new product being sold in stores everywhere? Writing the programs for a cool computer game? Working to save the environment? Designing the next generation of automobiles or aircraft? If you can imagine working in any of these or any other engineering career, keep your ambitions alive by learning what steps to take while you're still in school and developing the personal habits necessary to succeed."

WHERE TO START

If these engineering careers sound intriguing, you can get started during high school. Some classes will provide a solid base for future studies. Checking with your school's guidance counselor is a good place to start as far as exploring your options for classes. According to Engineering Your Future, there are certain classes that you should make sure that you take during high school. During ninth grade, take algebra I or geometry, some sort of physical science course, and English. In tenth grade, continue to algebra II, geometry, or applied math, as well as a biology course or an applied biology or chemistry course, as well as English. If you do not take algebra II during your sophomore year, then take it during eleventh grade or you can take an advanced algebra II course. Also take an advanced science course in chemistry or physics and another English course. In your senior year, take a higher math course, such as probability and statistics, calculus, or a college-level math course. This is also the time to take advanced physics or chemistry, as well as another year of English. By following these guidelines, you'll be giving yourself the best possible grounding for an engineering career.

If you're lucky enough to attend a high school that has a strong vo-tech department, you may also be able to take engineering-specific courses, such as pre-engineering, engineering technology basics, digital engineering, engineering design, civil engineering and architecture, aerospace engineering,

Many schools have vo-tech programs where girls can take engineering classes before even graduating from high school.

and computerized machining. Depending on what is offered by your high school's affiliated vo-tech school, you may be able to get some very specific engineering knowledge before you even get to college.

In addition to taking strong foundational classes, you should start developing the habits that will help throughout high school and then when you move into college: making a personal commitment to

VO-TECH

A vocational-technical school, often called a vo-tech or voc-tech school, is a school that concentrates on providing vocational and technical training to its students. This may be training that enables students to get a good job right out of high school, such as in construction trades or health care, or it might be training in advance for advanced education at the college level. Vo-tech schools are more vital than ever in a world where workers increasingly need technical skills. According to Steve DeWitt at the Association for Career and Technical Education in Alexandria, Virginia, "Eight out of ten 'jobs of the future' listed by the Bureau of Labor Statistics require training provided by career/technical education. The bulk of high-demand science, technology, engineering and mathematics (STEM) jobs require middle-level workers—for instance, the technicians who keep wind energy sites running."

doing well in school, prioritizing, using your time well, developing concentration and focus, following through on commitments, and learning how to work well with other students and with teachers. Stacey DelVecchio describes how she made high school work for her:

> I loved school. I created good study habits, which really helped me in the long run. I was in honors math and science, but this was in no way a requirement for going into engineering. I think the good study habits were more critical. I think it's also important to learn whatever you can when you're in high school. Don't worry about graduating early or anything like that. Take what's available, especially in math and science, and put your whole heart into it.

High school may also offer extracurricular activities that work well for tech girls interested in engineering. These could include Lego Mindstorms or First Robotics clubs, where teams design and program robots and compete against other teams on a national scale. Some schools have engineering clubs, which can include visits to local companies that utilize engineers. Your school might also sponsor science fairs or contests, where students compete with technical or science-related projects. And don't forget about vacations—some schools even offer camps for students who are interested in robotics, computer programming, and other tech-related topics. Take full advantage of the opportunities that your school has to offer, both for gaining knowledge and as a way to get a taste of different

An education in engineering fields may include learning to design or operate tools for assembling machines in a manufacturing plant assembly line.

types of engineering and decide what you find to be the most appealing.

Your community may also have opportunities for students interested in engineering. If you live near a college campus, keep your eyes and ears open for camps or classes that might be offered for young people. Some communities also sponsor camps, especially in the summer. Or there may be local organizations of engineers and employers who mentor budding engineers through factory visits. These might also be a gateway for internships or job-shadowing experiences with engineers who work in your community. It's a great way to gain firsthand experience and really see what it's like to be an engineer.

MORE THAN CAMPFIRES AND CANOES

For just a taste of what camps can offer tech girls who are interested in engineering, the Pathways to Science website lists some summer opportunities. It includes camps where teens can assist in research at the Science and Engineering Apprenticeship Program at a Department of Navy laboratory, a CompuGirls camp for girls interested in computer science, science research opportunities at Baylor University, and the BlueStamp Engineering program for teens in New York City, Houston, and San Francisco, where professional engineers supervise students in real-world engineering projects. And these are just a few of many possibilities.

ON TO COLLEGE

As high school comes to an end, it's important to find a college that offers a solid engineering program. You will most likely take either the SAT or the ACT test in your junior or senior year, but it's important to choose a school and take the test that it requires for admission. Again, your guidance counselor can help you with this, particularly in identifying good schools. And it's also important to visit schools and ask questions, especially of women who have attended these schools and graduated with engineering degrees. Ideally, the school's engineering program should also include plenty of opportunities for co-oping, which is a term for alternating classroom time with periods of experience in an actual workplace. DelVecchio explains how important this was to her engineering career:

> In my second year of school, I had my first co-op job and continued to gain 1.5 years of on-the-job experience during my five years at UC [University of Cincinnati]. These co-op experiences helped me understand, at least a little, what it meant to be an engineer. That kept me engaged, especially as the engineering classes were fairly theoretical at times. I can't imagine getting an engineering degree without co-oping, especially for someone in my situation, who really didn't know what engineering was.

There may also be work-study and internship opportunities in the engineering field, which is why it's vital to choose a college where engineering is one of the strongest majors.

And don't forget that there may be special grants and scholarships available for young women who want to study engineering. There are many organizations dedicated to fostering women in the engineering field, and they may provide special scholarships.

It's tough to decide just what engineering career appeals the most. Be sure to take a tour of some of these careers and get a better idea of what they're really like.

Chapter two

NOT YOUR GRANDFATHER'S ENGINEERING JOB

The careers that most people think of when they think of "engineer" are those where older men with pocket protectors and slide rules design cumbersome machines using pencils and drafting boards. This might have been true when your grandfather was young, but not now. The three classic categories of engineers—mechanical, civil, and electrical—are just as relevant today than ever before. And they all use up-to-the-minute technology and tools. In a world where changing climates, growing populations, and new technologies affect every aspect of daily life, these kinds of engineers are also desperately needed, both now and in the immediate future.

FROM DESIGN TO CONSTRUCTION

Mechanical engineers are the ones who not only design the products and machines that we use every day, but they also make sure that they can be manufactured and make improvements to them

Mechanical engineers often work in the automotive industry, designing better, more efficient engines for vehicles.

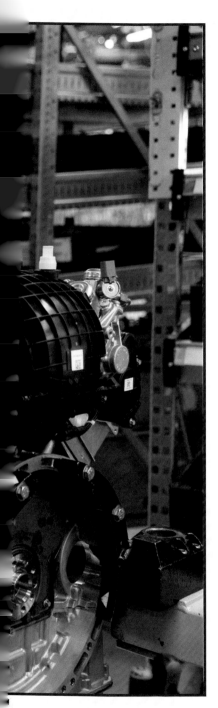

when necessary. According to the Columbia University School of Engineering, "Mechanical engineering is a diverse subject that derives its breadth from the need to design and manufacture everything from small individual parts and devices ([such as] microscale sensors and inkjet printer nozzles) to large systems ([such as] spacecraft and machine tools). The role of a mechanical engineer is to take a product from an idea to the marketplace." A mechanical engineer needs to have specific skills and knowledge to do such a comprehensive job. She has to think about the forces, such as extreme temperatures or high pressure or moisture, which might affect a product or part. Then she needs to design the product to cope with these forces and yet still be functional and user-friendly as well as sturdy and dependable.

Because these skills are needed for almost any product that is manufactured, the mechanical engineer is probably the most diverse discipline in engineering. Mechanical engineers work in the automotive industry, aerospace, and biotechnology. They also work with computers and electronics, energy, environmental controls, automation and robotics, and manufacturing. Mechanical engineers even work with the "machine" that is the human body. For this reason, there are thirty-six different technical division in the American Society of Mechanical Engineers (ASME)!

Female engineers work in the shipping industry, designing ships and navigation systems.

BUILDING BRIDGES . . . AND MUCH MORE

Civil engineering is the branch of engineering that deals with the construction of projects such as

roads, bridges, tunnels, power plants and other energy systems, water systems, ports, railroads, and airports. Basically, civil engineering deals with the built environment, and it is the oldest form of engineering. When the first people put a log across a river to make it easier to cross or built a roof for shelter, they were acting as the first civil engineers. According to the American Society of Civil Engineers, "Civil engineers touch many aspects of our everyday lives. From the water you use to brush your teeth in the morning to the road you drive on to work and the school where you take your children to the power that charges your cell phone."

However, civil engineers do much more than design and build bridges and tunnels. They are found in many other industries as well, such as aerospace, the automotive and shipbuilding industries, and the power industry. Basically, they can be found wherever facilities need to be constructed. Civil engineers will design those facilities and then often serve as construction managers to make sure that their ideas are built correctly.

FROM NURSE TO ENGINEER

Lisa Brothers is a successful civil engineer, but it was a choice that she needed a little help to make. In high school, when she was trying to decide on a career path, her school's guidance counselor urged her to try nursing, but it actually was her typing teacher who gave her the idea for engineering, as she explains in this interview with the American Society of Civil Engineers:

"I was taking typing. And my typing teacher said to me, Lisa, you're good in math, you're good in science. What about engineering? And I thought about it, and because of her I researched what an engineer did, and basically applied to undergraduate school for engineering." Today Lisa works at Judith Nitsch Engineering, Inc., in Boston, Massachusetts.

NO CROSSED WIRES HERE

Electrical engineers deal with the fields of electronics, electricity, and electromagnetism. This is a pretty broad category, and it spans the smallest handheld device to the largest complex supercomputer. According to the Sokanu career testing company:

> Electrical engineering deals with electricity, electro-magnetism and electronics. It also covers power, control systems, telecommunications and signal processing. These engineers are usually concerned with

large-scale electrical systems such as motor control and power transmission, as well as utilizing electricity to transmit energy. Electrical engineers may work on a diverse range of technologies, from the design of household appliances, lighting and wiring of buildings, telecommunication systems, electrical power stations and satellite communications. They may plan their designs using computer-aided software or they may also sketch ideas by hand.

Electrical engineering, like every engineering discipline, is broken up into smaller concentrations or specialties, including microelectronics, signal processing, power, controls, telecommunications, instrumentation, and electronics.

WOMEN IN ENGINEERING

How do the numbers measure up for women in civil and mechanical types of engineering? According to the U.S. Bureau of Labor Statistics, right now women make up about 13 percent of the workforce in engineering. Civil engineering in particular is a growing field, and women are earning more civil engineering degrees every year. They are also earning more of the master's and doctoral level degrees in this field. This puts them in an ideal position to meet a rapidly expanding career field.

GETTING THERE

Becoming a mechanical, civil, or electrical engineer requires a four-year bachelor's degree for an entry-level job. In most states, engineers are also required to be licensed if they are going to sell their services to the public. To conduct research, these engineering specialties require a master's degree. Some colleges and universities have programs where students can attend for five or six years and earn a bachelor's and a master's degree. Often these programs combine study with practical work experience, which lets engineers learn and also make money to pay for school at the same time.

There are also apprenticeships available for engineering students, usually with larger, established companies. These provide the opportunity for hands-on work in a particular field and possibilities for advancement. Depending on the job, they may require that you already have a four-year college degree, but in some cases they can be done while you are still attending college.

Chapter three

GETTING YOUR HANDS DIRTY

*B*ut perhaps you're looking for an engineering career that involves more getting your hands dirty and less theory and design. Being green is very popular today: cultivating renewable sources of energy, preserving the environment, and dealing with climate change. For girls who are interested in both engineering and the environment, there are engineering careers that might be a perfect fit. Environmental engineering is not new, but it has many new applications in a world where the environment is of growing concern, and questions about how we will cope with a changing physical world are becoming more insistent.

WHAT DO THEY DO?

An environmental engineer's work can cover many different types of jobs. According to the Science Buddies website, "Environmental engineers plan projects around their city or state—such as municipal water systems, landfills, recycling centers, or sanitation facilities—that are essential to the health of people who live there. Environmental engineers also work to minimize the impact of human developments,

Many new buildings now have green roofs, which require engineers to make sure they can support the weight of growing vegetation and handle water effectively.

such as new roads or dams, on environments and habitats, and they strive to improve the quality of our air, land, and water."

An environmental engineer might be hired to design a new water system and wastewater treatment facilities for a growing community. Or in a location with limited fresh water, they might design a desalination plant to turn saltwater into fresh water for agricultural irrigation without harming marine life. Perhaps they will find a way to reduce the toxic emission from power plants that harm the environment and contribute to acid rain and air pollution. Or they might work in construction, designing green roofs (roofs with grass and other plants growing on them) to reduce energy loss and increase natural cooling and insulation.

Environmental engineers often create a bridge between principles of science and mathematics and affordable, efficient applications of those principles in real-world technical problems. They use knowledge of biology and chemistry to solve environmental problems with pollution, recycling, waste disposal, and public health. They might have to evaluate plans for these types of facilities and advise on the environmental effects. They might also research the potential effects of a construction project on the environment, analyzing scientific and environmental data and even performing tests during the project to make sure that regulations are being followed. They may also act as consultants for protecting wildlife and lessening influences on air and water quality for certain types of projects. Finally, they might have to consult on projects where previous environmental damage is being cleaned up.

Because the job description for an environmental engineer is so varied, the workplace setting can be wide-ranging, too. An environmental engineer might work in an office, lab, or industrial plant, or outdoors at a construction site. Many of these engineers travel across the country or even around the world to different project locations.

MEET KATY DEACON

In 2007, Katy Deacon of England earned the title of Young Woman Engineer of the year. Katy works in energy engineering, although she started her career by working in aeronautical engineering at British Airways. But she soon found that she was interested in energy. She spoke with the *Independent* newspaper in England, explaining how an extracurricular engineering program in college led her to explore a career in renewable energy. When she was asked why it's important for women to become engineers as well as men, Katy responded, "Whether you are a woman or a man, you share your different skills to create the solution for the client. As long as you have got the training and can actually do the work then there's no problem. Only about 6 percent of engineers are women. Engineers are supposed to create solutions (for the public at large), but what those statistics show is that men are creating all the solutions. Having women in engineering is important because it allows a different perspective."

WHAT'S INSIDE?

Environmental engineering deals with the outside world, whereas materials engineering deals with the inside world, the materials that make up many objects and even the human body. And while they may be concerned with materials on a microscopic level, their work can also involve finding ways to adapt existing materials in an environmentally friendly way. For example, a materials engineer might develop a new

Engineers use their imaginations to create innovative ways to reuse products, such as this park bench made from recycled plastic.

method of recycling old non-metal computer parts into items such as sewer grates, park benches, or fences. Perhaps they research ways to create cars with ceramic engines instead of metal, which allows them to be lighter and more fuel-efficient, and thus more environmentally friendly. Or they might explore ways to take the natural glue made by sea mussels and adapt it into a new industrial adhesive. But they may go inside the human body as well, creating new materials for body parts such as replacement joints. Basically everything in our environment is made of chemicals, and a materials engineer explores ways to use those chemical properties to improve existing materials or create new ones.

Most materials engineers specialize in a particular kind of material, such as ceramics or metals. Materials engineers usually do their work in a laboratory doing research and development, creating new material or doing tests on raw materials or finished products. They are often employed in industries such as manufacturing, where improved or new materials are often needed.

ENGINEERING ENERGY

One of the most in-demand engineering careers in the environmental category is energy engineering. An energy engineer can help buildings, including homes, factories, and municipal and office buildings, use energy more efficiently and reduce the amount of energy they need. They might also help to reduce the amount of greenhouse gases being released into the atmosphere, which contributes to climate change. An energy engineer might make recommendations in an office building for replacing traditional light sources with more energy-efficient lamps and ballasts. They might use an infrared camera to do an energy audit of a home or business building, to see where heat is being lost. They could analyze a production line in a factory and make recommendations for using energy more efficiently. Or they might review the architectural plan for a new building and make suggestions for improving the heating and cooling efficiency. Basically, an energy engineer might be called in at any stage of a building's or home's lifespan, either when it is being constructed or when it is being remodeled for energy efficiency. Energy engineers might also work within a corporation to educate and encourage employees in energy reduction and conservation.

Energy engineers work within buildings to do energy audits, but they might also work outside at construction projects. If they conduct energy audits, they might travel frequently to conduct them in businesses and offices beyond their local area.

WHAT DO YOU NEED TO KNOW?

These environmentally related engineering jobs require similar educational backgrounds and at least a bachelor's degree, although materials science research most often requires a master's degree or higher. In high school, a tech girl should take courses in biology, chemistry, and physics, as well as computer science and statistics. A student specifically interested in environmental engineering would also benefit from classes in environmental science and marine biology, if her school offers them. In addition, an environmental engineering career requires a love of the outdoors and an interest in the good of the community. Energy engineers should be detail-oriented and have excellent communication skills, especially if they have to negotiate between what a builder wants and what's best for the project's energy efficiency. A materials engineer benefits from curiosity and perseverance as well as liking to do hands-on experiments.

Projected job growth for these engineering focuses varies. Materials engineers are in average demand right now, but environmental and energy engineers are expected to see above-average job growth, reflecting the increasing importance of energy use and environmental protection.

Chapter four

THE MAD SCIENTIST'S LAB

*P*erhaps your engineering interests aren't so much about getting your hands dirty in the field, but rather getting them dirty in a lab instead. Maybe your idea of fun is chemistry or biology lab class. Those who enjoy research and want to help the environment or save energy might enjoy discovering new products or processes rather than getting out there in the field. These three types of engineering careers rely heavily on research and experimentation: chemical engineering, biomedical engineering, and bioengineering.

A GIANT CHEMISTRY SET

Did you have a chemistry set when you were little or love chemistry class in high school? Then you may be ripe for a career as a chemical engineer. Although they have some overlap with a materials engineer, a chemical engineer not only develops new materials but also uses chemistry to change existing chemicals or materials so that they can be used in new and different ways or to solve problems. A chemical engineer may experiment with new ways to recycle things, such as plastic bottles into fabric for

A chemical engineer might be involved in creating a new formula for bubble gum that makes bigger, better bubbles.

clothing, or create new fuels to use in space travel. They might also do something fun, such as invent a new bubble gum formula that blows bigger bubbles more easily, or create a substance that can make different fluorescent colors at different temperatures. Maybe you'll invent a new food additive that makes processed food healthier, or a new type of paper that doesn't destroy trees. Chemical engineers might also work on a microscopic level with nanomaterials

If you loved the chemistry set you had as a child, or look forward to your high school chemistry classes, then being a chemical engineer might be perfect for you.

(materials that are measured in billionths of a meter, or nanometers) or with specific process such as oxidation. They might also create safety routines and procedures for workers who operate equipment or work closely with chemical reactions. Basically, chemical engineers are developing useful products and safeguarding health for people everywhere.

Although most chemical engineers work in a laboratory setting, perhaps for a company or at a research facility or university, there are others who spend some time out in the field, conducting tests at construction sites or places where oil and gas exploration is taking place.

What does it take to be a chemical engineer? Persistence, curiosity, and naturally, excellent skills in the chemistry lab. They also need good problem-solving skills. But you don't have to be a genius to become a chemical engineer. As Stacey DelVecchio, who has worked in chemical engineering for Caterpillar, Inc., says:

> A person who is technically curious makes a great engineer. They need to be able to think analytically and be good at problem solving. They can't be afraid of math and science. There's a myth out there that engineers have to be math and science wizzes. This is not the case. They need to understand math and science. They need to be able to solve problems. Engineers do not have to be math and science prodigies though. If you could take all this and give that budding engineer great communication skills, you'd have my perfect engineer.

CHEMISTRY + BIOLOGY = BIOCHEMICAL ENGINEER

Another type of engineer that's closely related to a chemical engineer is a biochemical engineer. Chemical engineers work with chemicals in many different applications and industries, but a biochemical engineer is concerned with chemicals in nature and the human body. Biochemical engineers might improve an existing medicine or create a new kind of fertilizer that will make it possible to grow bigger or better crops. They might work on ways to grow large batches of mammal cells to use for testing cancer drugs. Or they might create a mixture of ingredients to make a snack product healthier or better-tasting. They can take a recipe that has been formulated by a chemist or a biologist in the laboratory, and then find a way to adapt it to a large-scale manufacturing process. Biochemical engineers often work directly on making a large amount of a product for human use, but they are also concerned with the safety of the manufacturing plant and the products it makes.

Biochemical engineering also has several specializations. Metabolic engineers use genetics and molecules to make the production of metabolites and proteins more effective. Enzyme engineers design catalysts, which are agents that can produce chemicals and biochemicals. And tissue engineers study all the ways that living cells can be transplanted to help fight diseases.

Most biochemical engineers work in laboratories or industrial manufacturing plants, with limited time spent out in the field. Important skills for biochemical

MEET RAQUEL WIDRIG

Raquel Widrig works for Genentech as an engineer in manufacturing sciences. Her work involves developing processes such as cell cultures for new pharmaceutical drugs to be used in treating heart attacks and cystic fibrosis. She talks about what she likes best about her work in an interview with Careercornerstone.org: "The charter of Genentech is to provide pharmaceuticals for large unmet medical needs. I'm happy to be part of that because I'm actually on the process development end of developing the drug. So I have a real impact on making the drugs so that we can sell them to people who need them."

engineers include excellent problem-solving abilities, curiosity, the ability to work well in a team, and of course, mechanical and lab skills. They must have a good grounding, starting in high school, in physics, chemistry, biology, geometry, and calculus.

ENGINEERING + BIOLOGY + MEDICINE = BIOMEDICAL ENGINEER

Another related engineering field is biomedical engineering, which combines engineering, medicine, and biology, as well as fieldwork, research, and problem solving. Biomedical engineers might invent a better heart valve replacement or a new type of flexible artificial disc to replace damaged discs in

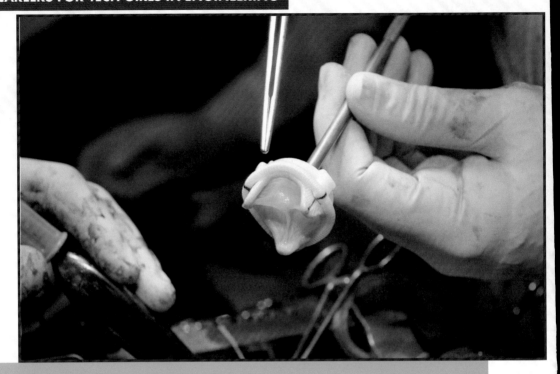

Biomedical engineers use engineering to solve problems in the body, such as inventing a new type of replacement heart valve.

the human spine. Or perhaps they are working on better and safer ultrasound technology for monitoring babies before they are born. Or they may create a better insulin pump for diabetics. Biomedical engineers use engineering to solve problems in medicine, by creating replacement body parts, new ways to administer drugs, or new medical instruments or testing equipment. They work to improve the quality of people's lives.

A biomedical engineer needs to be responsible and self-motivated, and must have have excellent communication skills, because they often act as go-betweens linking other types of engineers and

MEET KATIE HILPISCH

Katie Hilpisch works for Medtronic, helping invent new technologies for heart patients. She divides her work time between desk work on a computer and work in the lab. "My job is all about math and medicine!" she says on the Science Buddies blog. For Katie, being a biomedical engineer is basically figuring out the right combinations of science and possible answers that will improve a patient's quality of life. "Hands down, I most enjoy helping patients. It is very rewarding to come to work every day and get the chance to do something that helps people who are sick."

physicians. Above all, they must be interested in helping people by solving medical problems. In addition to taking classes in biology, chemistry, physics, and math, a high school student interested in biomedical engineering should also take physiology, biotechnology, and statistics if those classes are available. Most biomedical engineers have advanced college degrees, and many may actually have a medical doctor's degree.

All three of these laboratory and research-heavy engineering careers are in demand right now, either because they cross over into many other fields that use chemistry and biochemistry or because they are part of the growing field of health care and medicine.

Chapter five

YOUR INNER INVENTOR

Maybe you like the idea of inventing new products but not necessarily in a lab or in the areas of biology or chemistry. Have you imagined how you could invent something to make life easier? Or stood in line at an airport check-in and wondered how to design automation that would make the whole

When you bite into your favorite snack, remember that an industrial design engineer likely invented the packaging that kept it fresher longer.

process faster and easier? Or struggled to open a favorite snack, and puzzled over a better way to keep food fresh without requiring sharp tools to open the package? Working as an industrial engineer or an industrial design engineer might be a great fit.

IMPROVING THE OLD WITH NEW IDEAS

Industrial engineers are good at coming up with new ways to handle existing problems. For example, they might make it faster and cheaper to manufacture cars by designing better assembly lines. Or they might work on how to transport perishable goods such as frozen food across the country in the fastest way possible, even when the weather is bad. Or they can apply their problem-solving skills to designing better operating rooms in hospitals, making it easier, faster, and safer for doctors, nurses, and patients. These are all areas where industrial engineers can make a difference in everyday lives. According to ScienceBuddies.org:

> You've probably heard the expression "build a better mousetrap." Industrial engineers are the people who figure out how to do things better. They find ways that are smarter, faster, safer, and easier, so that companies become more efficient, productive, and profitable, and employees have work environments that are safer and more rewarding. You might think from their name that industrial engineers just work for big manufacturing companies, but they are employed in a wide range of industries,

including the service, entertainment, shipping, and healthcare fields. For example, nobody likes to wait in a long line to get on a roller coaster ride, or to get admitted to the hospital. Industrial engineers tell companies how to shorten these processes. They try to make life and products better—finding ways to do more with less is their motto.

An industrial engineer is the bridge between scientific discoveries and commercial applications

Engineers take scientific principles and apply them to the real world. They may figure out how to make roller coasters even more exciting and yet keep them safe.

that meet the needs of consumers and society. They begin with a problem and then decide the most effective ways to use the basic ingredients of production (people, machines, materials,

VOICES FROM THE FIELD

When asked why they became industrial engineers (IEs), many people working in the field mentioned the opportunities to work with people and not just machines. According to the Institute of Industrial Engineers, many industrial engineers feel that their jobs are more people-related than most engineering jobs. There is more opportunity for interaction. As one engineer said, "I liked the fact that IEs have a technical aspect to their work but also deal with people and the business side. It's not just hard-core technical work but focuses on integrating people with systems. It also is a diverse career with seemingly limitless options on different types of jobs."

information, and energy) to either create a product or provide a service.

Becoming an industrial engineer requires the same kinds of aptitudes that most engineering careers require: good math, logic, and communication skills. But it also requires an interest in both engineering and business, and an ability to look at the big picture of a situation while still being able to study and analyze the small details.

Industrial engineers need to have, at minimum, a bachelor's degree. There are graduate degrees in industrial engineering, but these are mostly for people who decide to work in colleges and universities. The best way to prepare during high school is to take classes in biology, chemistry, physics, computer science, and math, as well as statistics and business classes if possible.

THE ARTISTIC ENGINEER

If you're interested in the jobs that an industrial engineer might do but want to focus even more closely on designing packaging, consider a packaging engineer career. These engineers work with companies to make their packaging both cost-effective and functional. They choose the materials, machinery, and production methods for creating the packaging, and try to eliminate unnecessary waste and expense.

Commercial and industrial packaging engineers might also work on designing better medicine bottles that are childproof but still easy for adults to open. They might also use special software called computer-aided design (CAD) tools or make physical models of new products before they go into production. Industrial design engineers can work on almost any type of manufactured good, and it's especially appealing to people who have an eye for art and design. Commercial and industrial designers have a good eye for balance, form, and attractiveness. They create packaging and product design for many different types of products, from cars to toys to sporting goods to high-tech

Industrial packaging designers help protect young children from poisoning when they create childproof medication bottles.

equipment. These engineers create products that are not only functional but also beautiful.

Designers work with manufacturers and companies that produce goods. First they meet to get an idea of what they are being asked to design, as well as the specific requirements, and then they do research into the product and how it will be used. The next step is to develop a new design or alter an existing one, based on the input and research, and to use computers or hand-drawn sketches to create sketches and diagrams for the new product. They work with the company again to see if the design works and is cost-effective, and make any necessary adjustments before the product is actually manufactured.

GETTING THERE

Like other engineers, industrial design engineers have strong aptitude in math, problem solving, and science, but they also have creativity, imagination, good fine-motor skills, an artistic eye, and good communication skills. Subjects to study in high school include the usual science and math classes, and art, applied technology, and drafting, if your school provides these classes. A bachelor's degree is required, but most industrial designers have a master's degree in industrial design. Some designers even earn a master's degree in business administration to help them in their work environment.

Designers also have to stay current with tastes, styles, and trends in design, because these can change quickly. They also need to be good at com-municating their ideas both visually and verbally, as well as in writing.

Chapter six

GOING HIGH TECH... IT'S NOT JUST FOR GEEKS

If advanced technology seems intriguing, then there's one more category of engineering to consider: high-tech computer, software, and aviation/aerospace engineering. Engineers receive a lot of well-deserved credit and attention in the high-tech industries. This includes not only aviation and aerospace, designing airplanes and space vehicles, but also in computers and software engineering. These are career areas where engineers are in high demand, but they are also areas that require constant, continuing education and training to stay current.

FLYING HIGH...AND HIGHER

Imagine working for NASA or for a big aircraft manufacturer like Boeing, finding ways to design better vehicles or systems for air travel or space travel. Think about working on a team that's preparing for the next space shuttle flight to service the International Space Station or the

High-tech software and computer engineers are working to create satellite technology for using cell phones in areas without regular cell service.

Hubble Telescope. Or working on a satellite for communications or for mapping or monitoring certain parts of the earth. Picture developing new satellite phone technology for places where there's no cell phone service. Or visualize designing a new airplane wing that makes aircraft more maneuverable. These are all things that someone might do as an aerospace engineer. Aerospace engineers design, develop, and then test all kinds of aircraft, space vehicles, and even missiles, and then supervise when they reach the manufacturing stage. These engineers are divided into two categories: aeronautical engineers

The astronautical engineers at the National Aeronautics and Space Administration (NASA) designed the new Orion spacecraft, which, unlike older space capsules, can be reused for multiple flights.

work on aircraft, and astronautical engineers work on spacecraft. In addition, they might specialize in certain types of vehicles, such as commercial airliners, fighter jets, or rockets, or they might work only on instrumentation, guidance, navigation propulsion, or control systems.

NASA engineers worked to create a new reusable space capsule for future space flights. Unlike the old Apollo capsules, which were designed to land in the ocean and were usually damaged or destroyed by the saltwater, the new

Orion crew capsules can be reused for more than one flight. Thanks to astronautical engineering, the successful gumdrop shape of the Apollo capsule has been redesigned for the future.

Aerospace and aviation engineers can work in a variety of industries and settings: sometimes in laboratories or research facilities, in commercial companies, or even outside at test sites or construction sites. They are also in demand.

GETTING THERE

An entry-level job in aerospace or aviation engineering requires at least a bachelor's degree. Many start with an engineering degree in mechanical engineering or a related field and then earn a graduate degree in aeronautics or aviation to conduct research or obtain higher-level jobs. It is especially important that students interested in this type of engineering have high school courses in math and science, computer science, applied technology, and statistics. You should also be creative, curious, and detail-oriented, and be able to analyze situations and come up with solutions. Good communication skills are also helpful because many aerospace and aviation projects are done as a team.

KEYBOARDS AND HARDWARE AND SOFTWARE, OH MY

Being a computer or software engineer is much more than just being good at using computers.

Engineering programs for students, such as those that use the Lego Mindstorms robotics system, are a great way to become familiar with engineering processes and designs.

These engineers apply both scientific theory and engineering design to computers and use it to improve both computer hardware and the software that runs them. They write new software programs to solve problems or create more efficient ways to do things. They might also write new software for new computer hardware devices such as robots or other automated systems. According to engineergirl.org, this might include the following:

- Design a feather-light laptop
- Develop the necessary systems for running the latest electrical car
- Oversee the computer network for a telecommunications company
- Invent a brand-new video game
- Develop the control systems for a large-scale robotic manufacturing plant
- Create a new operating system for personal computers

Computer and software engineers also have the advantage of often being able to telecommute, or work from home. They might work for one particular company or as contractors, moving from job to job with different companies. And both computer and software engineers are in high demand and earn good salaries for their work.

GETTING THERE

The ideal computer or software engineers want to keep getting better at things and are not content to reach a certain point and stay there. They can think creatively and actually enjoy big challenges. They are as happy working in a team as they are with working alone, and they can be patient and focused. They have to be able to remember details and important facts, and they should be interested in computer modeling.

These engineers have a bachelor's degree for entry-level jobs and generally specialize in either computer hardware or software specifically. But even once they have landed a job, it is vital that they keep their skills current, continue training, and always know the latest

WHAT'S EXCITING ABOUT ENGINEERING?

Celia Gonzalez works as a computer engineer for ATT Services. When asked why she chose a career in engineering, she told Engineergirl.com the following:

(1) My dad was an immigrant who helped the rest of our family establish their careers, most of them in engineering, but he did not. He always worked in engineering jobs since he was ten-twelve years old, but never went to school for that. I wanted to help realize the dream he had. I became the first female engineer in my family that I'm aware of.

(2) My high school science teacher asked a very simple question, "Have you ever thought about engineering?" She believed in me and helped me enroll in a small internship that gave me hands-on, research-oriented, and interactive exposure to engineering. They made engineering something fascinating, fun, and something a high schooler could understand. Celia was lucky to have a supportive teacher to help her not only achieve her career goal but also realize her family's dream as well. Her story also shows that it's possible to become a female engineer no matter what kind of support systems you have.

technical developments in hardware or programming languages or other areas of computer science. In high school, students need to take courses in math and science, computer science, and electronics if possible.

And the more "geek" skills you have, the better, so join the computer club if your school has one or volunteer to work with your school's IT person to troubleshoot and solve computer issues.

THE SKY'S THE LIMIT

If you are a dedicated tech girl and interested in engineering, it's pretty clear that there are many fields and focuses in engineering careers and one of them is bound to appeal to you. So it's off to college, and in four short years, you could have a fresh engineering degree. And then what?

Chapter seven

IT'S OFF TO WORK WE GO

High school graduation has come and gone. You spent another four years of college working hard and earning an engineering degree in the field that you're most interested in. It's time to find a job and put that degree to work.

MAKING CONNECTIONS

If you are lucky, you have attended a college that has internships and other workplace experience programs in place. Stacey DelVecchio emphasized how attending a school with a co-op program, where students went out into the workplace to gain engineering experience, helped her: "Off I went to college to study chemical engineering without really understanding what a chemical engineer did day in and day out. I'm sure this is a common leap of faith that many potential engineers do. My huge advantage was that I went to the University of Cincinnati (UC), which required all engineering students to co-op." Internships and job co-op

Hands-on engineering experience, such as learning to use a 3D printer, is a valuable part of interning or job sharing in existing engineering companies.

experiences provide hands-on experience in what engineers really do, as well as what types of engineering are the most appealing. They can also provide valuable networking opportunities. You can make connections with the people in the company, and in some cases, interns may be offered a job with the company upon graduation. And even if the company does not offer you a job, there are mentors there who worked with you and might be willing to provide a reference for you as you begin job-hunting.

There are some other things that you can do while you are still in college that will help when it's time to find a job. According to Lynn Jacobs and Jeremy Hyman, these include participating in any kind of hands-on learning project that you can find and creating a portfolio of your work from these opportunities. You should also work in teams as much as possible to demonstrate that you can work well in a group, even if it is a sports team or as part of the school newspaper or an academic team. Summer internships are also very valuable not only for experience and connections for future work but also for adding more projects to your portfolio.

WHERE ARE THEY GOING?

Although women are increasingly working in engineering and other STEM (science, technology, engineering, and mathematics) fields, they are 45 percent more likely than men to leave those careers within a year, according to research by the Center for Talent Innovation. Why? Some women say it's a sense of isolation because there are still so many more men in the field. Others say it has to do with overly critical feedback, and others say it's the lack of other female engineer mentors and sponsors. But many companies are starting dedicated programs to help their female STEM-career employees and keep them more satisfied with their work and workplace.

Looking for a first real engineering job is much like looking for any other job. The school's career placement office should not only offer job openings and opportunities to its students but also workshops and assistance with writing a résumé and cover letter and how to prepare for a job interview. There are also many online job searching sites that list current openings in all fields, including engineering.

YOU'RE HIRED! NOW WHAT?

With perseverance and hard work, the day will come when you hear the magic words "You're hired!" and you've gotten your first engineering job. It might seem like your problems are over and everything

Even after getting a job in the engineering industry, keep networking, brainstorming, and collaborating with other engineers.

will be clear sailing from now on, but there are still things to keep in mind and things to watch out for. It is important to keep networking with other engineers, either in your workplace or by joining national organizations for engineers. There are special organizations for women engineers, which can be especially helpful for support and help if you decide to search for a new job or are struggling with issues of workplace discrimination. Bias against women engineers is gradually fading, but it can still be present at times. As Stacey DelVecchio said concerning her experience with discrimination as a female engineer, "In the workplace, I did start to see some bias. I don't think I'd say it was as strong as negativity though. There have just been some times where the environment wasn't as inclusive as it could be. This is the main reason why I've devoted so much of my time to the Society of Women Engineers and being an advocate for diversity. We need all our engineers to feel like they belong."

Teamwork is also important because many engineering projects are conducted by groups of engineers and not just one working alone. This is where communication skills will be especially useful, both to communicate orally and to express your ideas in writing and visually.

You've arrived at the engineering career of your dreams. At the very least, you've taken the first step along your career path, because sometimes it takes a while to find the perfect fit when it comes to careers. But there's more to being a tech girl in the engineering world than just doing your job.

Chapter eight

TECH GIRLS RULE

A chieving a career in a STEM field like engineering is an accomplishment, and one that needs to be maintained with continuing training and education. It's also important, especially for women who are working in fields that used to be for men only, to create and nurture good relationships with other women in similar situations. Like it or not, there still may be times when women face discrimination in engineering and other tech fields.

WOMEN AND STEM

Although women have made huge gains into scientific careers that were once reserved for men, the harsh reality is that sometimes women still face discrimination or harassment or even just fewer opportunities in these fields. According to an article, "Harassment in Science, Replicated," by Christie Aschwanden in the *New York Times*, "Scientists [were invited] to fill out an online questionnaire about their experiences with harassment and assault at field sites; they received 666 responses, three-quarters of them from women. More than half of the female respondents said they weren't taken seriously because of their gender, one in three had experienced delayed career advancement, and nearly half said they had not received credit for their ideas." Sometimes bias against women in fields such as engineering isn't even deliberate. But its presence makes it even more important for women in STEM careers to form alliances and support networks among other women in the field, as well as to encourage more young women to pursue STEM careers going forward.

According to the article "Challenges, Strategies for Women Pursuing STEM Careers" in *Science Daily,* Mary Jean Amon's study [of women pursing STEM careers] uncovered three themes that emerged as women examined the effects of gender stereotypes in STEM fields: career strategies, barriers to achievement, and buffering strategies. "Gender stereotypes manifest in a variety of ways in a work environment, such as conflicting role expectations, a lack of authority and a variety of small, interpersonal cues that signal the potential bias against women," writes Amon. "It is common for organizations to promote policies against blatant acts of discrimination and sexual harassment, but it is less common for them to recognize the unconscious acts of bias that frequently occur." The study revealed that social support systems—encouragement from research advisers as well as family and friends—played a key role in helping women overcome challenges in these male-dominated professions.

TIMES, THEY ARE A-CHANGING

Women in STEM professions such as engineering have a responsibility to support each other and also young women who are being encouraged to attain

While there is bias against women in the engineering field, female engineers are still making many vital contributions to engineering fields, such as the design of new robotic hands.

their own STEM careers. Hopefully this will change as today's tech girls are participating more in engineering, science, and tech classes and activities in their schools. If tomorrow's male engineers are already used to girls in their high school classes, they will be more likely to accept them unquestioningly in their careers. A high school student in New Hampshire said the following:

> *Sometimes it is difficult taking classes that are mainly geared towards males. Sometimes I feel as though I am less respected (not by the teachers, all teachers*

I have had have been extremely supportive). It becomes natural once you develop a friendship with most of the guys in your class because they begin to see you as an equal. I've never had any huge issue. Naturally, I feel as though I belong in a class like that because the area of study is what I am interested in. Usually in the beginning it is difficult, but once the guys gain respect for you and see that you can do things equally as well as they can, there I nothing that separates you from the rest of them.

Women can not only compete in any engineering field they want, they may even accomplish more than some of their male colleagues.

Engineering is one of the most exciting STEM fields to work in, and while women might still face animosity or even demeaning behavior from male colleagues, a knowledgeable and smart tech girl who has taken her education seriously will become a woman who can hold her own in the engineering field and may well surpass her male colleagues.

As Stacey DelVecchio says:

> It may be difficult to figure out what an engineer does, and that's normal. There are so many different kinds of engineers and we all do something a little different. However, we're all working to make the world a better place. Do ask questions. Do keep an open mind. Do pursue something you love. Do learn. Do [as the Society of Women Engineers says in its poster, Be That Engineer] "Be Silly; Be outrageous; Be strong; Be amazing; Just be you." Do not let anyone tell you that you don't belong. Do not assume you're being discriminated against if things get tough. Look around you and assess the environment.

Engineers change the world. Really.

Glossary

ACT The American College Testing assessment tests for high school students applying to college.

AEROSPACE The division of technology and industry having to do with aviation and space flight.

APPRENTICE Someone learning a skill from a trained employer and who agrees to work for a certain amount of time for reduced wages.

ASTRONAUTICS The science of the construction and operation of vehicles that travel in space.

BALLAST A device that limits the amount of current in an electrical circuit, especially in fluorescent lamps.

BIOMEDICAL Having to do with biology as well as medicine.

BIOTECHNOLOGY Using biological processes or manipulating living organisms for industrial reasons, such as producing pharmaceuticals.

CAD Short for computer-aided design, CAD is software that helps engineers and others create exact illustrations or designs.

CO-OP Alternating between time in the classroom and in a workplace.

DRAFTING The process of creating a mechanical drawing.

MENTOR A knowledgeable or dependable adviser, teacher, or trainer.

MICROSCALE On a very small scale; having to do with extremely small quantities.

MUNICIPAL Having to do with the government of a city or town.

NANOMATERIALS Substances that have the scale of billionths of a meter, or nanometers.

OXIDATION The result or process of combining any element with oxygen, such as burning or rusting.

PERISHABLE Something, especially food, that is likely to rapidly decay or go bad.

PHYSIOLOGY The division of biology that deals with processes of life or living organisms and their parts.

RENEWABLE Not depleted by being used, such as water, wind, or solar power.

SAT The Scholastic Aptitude Test, which is taken by high school students who are applying to college to test their academic skills.

STATISTICS The science of collecting and analyzing numerical data, especially for calculating percentages and numbers for a whole group based on a smaller sample.

STEM The academic disciplines of science, technology, engineering, and mathematics, especially in relation to education.

TELECOMMUTE To work from home, communicating by telephone, Internet, and e-mail.

WASTEWATER Any water that has been used for washing, flushing, or sewage purposes and must be treated before reuse.

For More Information

American Association of Engineering Societies
1801 Alexander Bell Drive
Reston, VA 20191
(888) 400-2237
Website: http://www.aaes.org
The American Association of Engineering Societies'
   mission is to serve as a voice to represent U.S.
   engineers and to advance their impact on the
   public.

American Society of Safety Engineers
1800 E. Oakton Street
Des Plaines, IL 60018
(847) 699-2929
Website: http://www.asse.org
The American Society of Safety Engineers is an
   organization for engineers who work in the areas
   of public health and safety.

Canadian Association for Girls in Science
6700 Century Avenue, Suite 100
Mississauga, ON L5N 6A4
Canada
(905) 567-7190
Website: http://www.cagis.ca
The purpose of CAGIS is to promote, educate, and
   support interest and confidence in STEM among
   girls.

IEEE Women in Engineering
3 Park Avenue, 17th Floor
New York, NY 10016-5997

(212) 419-7900
Website: http://www.ieee.org
The Institute of Electrical and Electronics Engineers
    is dedicated to promoting women engineers and
    scientists and inspiring girls around the world
    to follow their academic interests to a career in
    engineering.

International Network of Women Engineers and
    Scientists
Brock University
Department of Biological Sciences
500 Glenridge Avenue
St. Catharines, ON L2S 3A1
Canada
(905) 688-5550 ext.4023
Website: http://www.inwes.org
This organization's mission is "to build a better future
    worldwide through full and effective participation
    of women and girls in all aspects of Science,
    Technology, Engineering, and Mathematics."

Society for Canadian Women in Science and Technology
#311 – 525 Seymour Street
Vancouver, BC V6B 3H7
Canada
(604) 893-8657
Website: http://www.scwist.ca
The Society for Canadian Women in Science
    and Technology promotes, encourages,
    and empowers women and girls in science,
    engineering, and technology.

Society of Women Engineers
203 N. La Salle Street, Suite 1675
Chicago, IL 60601
(877) 793-4636
Website: http://societyofwomenengineers.swe.org
This organization represents women in all areas of
    engineering and encourages young women to
    become engineers.

Women in Engineering Proactive Network
1901 E. Asbury Street
Suite 220
Denver, CO 80210
(303) 871-4642
Website: http://www.wepan.org
The mission of Women in Engineering Proactive
    Network is to propel higher education to increase
    the number and advance the prominence of
    diverse communities of women in engineering.

WEBSITES

Because of the changing nature of Internet links,
Rosen Publishing has developed an online list of
websites related to the subject of this book. This site
is updated regularly. Please use this link to access
the list:

http://www.rosenlinks.com/TECH/Eng

For Further Reading

Anderson, Michael, ed. *Closer Look at Genes and Genetic Engineering*. New York, NY: Britannica Educational Publishing, 2011.

Baine, Celeste. *Is There an Engineer Inside You? A Comprehensive Guide to Career Decisions in Engineering*. Eugene, OR: Engineering Education Service Center, 2014.

Bix, Amy Sue. *Girls Coming to Tech! A History of American Engineering Education for Women*. Boston, MA: MIT Press, 2014.

Bow, James. *Electrical Engineering and the Science of Circuits*. St. Catharines, ON: Crabtree Publishing, 2013.

Cantú, Norma Elia. *Paths to Discovery: Chicanas with Careers in Science, Mathematics, and Engineering*. Los Angeles, CA: UCLA Chicano Studies Research Center Press, 2008.

Ferguson. *Careers in Focus: Engineering*. 3rd ed. New York, NY: Ferguson Publishing, 2007.

Hagler, Gina. *Top STEM Careers in Engineering* (Cutting-Edge STEM Careers). New York, NY: Rosen Publishing, 2014.

Hatch, Sybil E. *Changing Our World: True Stories of Women Engineers*. Reston, VA: American Society of Civil Engineers, 2006.

Hutson, Matt. *Cool Careers in Engineering*. San Diego, CA: Sally Ride Science, 2010.

Indovino, Shaina. *Women in Engineering*. Broomall, PA: Mason Crest, 2013.

Institute for Career Research. *Engineering and Technical Careers in Green Energy*. Chicago, IL: Institute for Career Research, 2012.

La Bella, Laura. *Internship & Volunteer Opportunities for People Who Love to Build Things.* New York, NY: Rosen Publishing, 2012.

Latham, Donna. *Bridges and Tunnels: Investigate Feats of Engineering with 25 Projects.* White River Junction, VT: Nomad Press, 2012.

Layne, Margaret E. *Women in Engineering: Pioneers and Trailblazers.* Reston, VA: American Society of Civil Engineers, 2009.

Layne, Margaret E. *Women in Engineering: Professional Life.* Reston, VA: American Society of Civil Engineers, 2009.

Lewis, Anna M. *Women of Steel and Stone: 22 Inspirational Architects, Engineers, and Landscape Designers.* Chicago, IL: Chicago Review Press, 2014.

Mooney, Carla. *Medical Technology and Engineering.* Chicago, IL: Britannica Digital Learning, 2014.

Rosser, Sue Vilhauer. *Breaking into the Lab: Engineering Progress for Women in Science.* New York, NY: New York University Press, 2012.

Schwartz, Heather E. *Cool Engineering Activities for Girls.* Minneapolis, MN: Capstone Press, 2012.

Solway, Andrew. *Civil Engineering and the Science of Structures.* St. Catharines, ON: Crabtree Publishing, 2012.

Van Cleave, Janice. *Janice VanCleave's Engineering for Every Kid: Easy Activities That Make Learning Science Fun.* New York, NY: Wiley, 2007.

Bibliography

American Society of Civil Engineers. "What Is Civil Engineering?" Retrieved October 3, 2014 (http://www.asce.org/What-Is-Civil-Engineering-/).

American Society of Civil Engineers. "Women in Civil Engineering: Contemporary Issues." Retrieved October 3, 2014 (http://www.asce.org/People-and-Projects/People/Womens-History/Women-in-Civil-Engineering—Contemporary-Issues/).

Aschwanden, Christie. "Harassment in Science, Replicated." *New York Times*, August 11, 2014. Retrieved October 2014 (http://www.nytimes.com/2014/08/12/science/harassment-in-science-replicated.html?_r=0).

Bureau of Labor Statistics, U.S. Department of Labor. "How to Become a Mechanical Engineer." Retrieved October 4, 2014 (http://www.bls.gov/ooh/architecture-and-engineering/mechanical-engineers.htm#tab-4).

Columbia Engineering. "What Is Mechanical Engineering?" Columbia University. Retrieved October 3, 2014 (http://me.columbia.edu/what-mechanical-engineering).

Cowen, Amy. "Biomedical Engineering and Heart Health." Sciencebuddies.org, October 3, 2011. Retrieved October 11, 2014 (http://www.sciencebuddies.org/blog/2011/10/biomedical-engineering-and-heart-health.php).

DelVecchio, Stacey (engineer for Caterpillar, Inc.). Interview with the author, October 8, 2014.

Education Portal. "Becoming a Packaging Engineer: Education and Career Roadmap." Retrieved

October 11, 2014 (http://education-portal.com/
articles/Become_a_Packaging_Engineer
_Education_and_Career_Roadmap.html).

Engineer Girl. "Computer Engineer." Retrieved
October 12, 2014 (http://www.engineergirl.org/
what_engineers_do/tryonacareer/6070.aspx).

Engineer Girl. "Interview: Celia Gonzalez." Retrieved
October 12, 2014 (http://www.engineergirl.org/
Engineers/interviews/22049.aspx).

Futures in Engineering. "Career Track." Engineering
Your Future. Retrieved October 3, 2014 (http://
www.futuresinengineering.com/career.php?id=10).

The Independent. "Interview: Katy Deacon, Young
Woman Engineer of the Year." May 14, 2007.
Retrieved November 17, 2014 (http://www
.independent.co.uk/student/magazines/
interview-katy-deacon-young-woman-engineer
-of-the-year-448814.html).

Jacobs, Lynn F., and Jeremy S. Hyman. "10 Tips
for Success for Engineering Students."
US News & World Report Education, December 2,
2009. Retrieved November 17, 2014 (http://www.
usnews.com/education/blogs/professors
-guide/2009/12/02/10-tips-for-success-for
-engineering-students-).

National Action Council for Minorities in Engineering.
"Types of Engineering." Retrieved October 3, 2014
(http://www.nacme.org/types-of-engineering).

Rappoport, Ann L. "Not Your Daddy's Vo Tech."
Metrokids. Retrieved October 3, 2014 (http://
www.metrokids.com/MetroKids/May-2011/Not
-Your-Daddy-039s-Vo-Tech/).

Science Buddies. "Aerospace Engineer: What Do They Do?" Retrieved October 12, 2014 (http://www.sciencebuddies.org/science-engineering-careers/engineering/aerospace-engineer).

Science Buddies. "Commercial/Industrial Designer: Key Facts and Information." Retrieved October 11, 2014 (http://www.sciencebuddies.org/science-engineering-careers/engineering/commercial-industrial-designer#keyfactsinformation).

Science Buddies. "Environmental Engineer: Key Facts and Information." Retrieved October 8, 2014 (http://www.sciencebuddies.org/science-engineering-careers/engineering/environmental-engineer#keyfactsinformation).

Science Buddies. "Industrial Engineer: Key Facts and Information." Retrieved October 10, 2014 (http://www.sciencebuddies.org/science-engineering-careers/engineering/industrial-engineer#keyfactsinformation).

Science Daily. "Challenges, Strategies for Women Pursuing STEM Careers." August 11, 2014. Retrieved October 30, 2014 (http://www.sciencedaily.com/releases/2014/08/140811124956.htm).

Sloan Career Cornerstone Center. "Profiles of Chemical Engineers: Raquel Widrig." Retrieved October 11, 2014 (http://www.careercornerstone.org/chemeng/profiles/widrig.htm).

Sloan Career Cornerstone Center. "Profiles of Civil Engineers: Lisa A. Brothers." Profiles of Civil Engineers. Retrieved October 3, 2014 (http://www.careercornerstone.org/pdf/civil/brothers.pdf).

Sokanu. "What Is an Electrical Engineer?" What Does an Electrical Engineer Do? Retrieved October 4, 2014 (https://www.sokanu.com/careers/electrical-engineer/).

Student (high school pre-engineering student). Interview with the author via Karen Fabianski, October 3, 2014.

Index

U

U.S. Bureau of Labor Statistics, 4, 11, 23

V

vo-tech schools, 10–11

W

Widrig, Raquel, 37
women in engineering, 4, 23, 28, 58
   bias/discrimination against, 59–60, 61–62, 65

ABOUT THE AUTHOR

Marcia Amidon Lusted is the author of more than 100 books and 450 magazine articles for young readers. She is also the editor of Cricket Media. In addition to writing for kids, she also works in sustainable development, an area where engineers are extremely important. She has also served as a judge for the national finals of the Future City competition, where students compete to design cities of the future and use many engineering principles.

PHOTO CREDITS

Cover © iStockphoto.com/sturti; cover and interior pages background image © iStockphoto.com/traffic_analyzer; cover and interior pages text banners © iStockphoto.com/slav; pp. 6, 64 Sigrid Gombert/Cultura/Getty Images; p. 8 Peter Cade/Iconica/Getty Images; p. 10 Jon Feingersh/Blend Images/ Getty Images; p. 13 Echo/Cultura/Getty Images; pp. 18–19 Tim Graham/Getty Images; pp. 20–21, 56–57 Thomas Barwick/ Stone/Getty Images; p. 26 Diane Cook and Len Jenshel/ National Geographic Image Collection/Getty Images; p. 29 Eunice Harris/Photolibrary/Getty Images; p. 33 Blasius Erlinger/ The Image Bank/Getty Images; p. 34 Purestock/Thinkstock; p. 38 Medicimage/Science Source; p. 40 Casey Rogers/ Invision/AP Images; p. 42 Sihasakprachum/Shutterstock.com; p. 45 Image Source/Getty Images; p. 48 Tim Robberts/Taxi/ Getty Images; p. 49 U.S. Navy/Getty Images; pp. 51, 63 © AP Images; p. 59 John Fedele/Blend Images/Getty Images.

Designer: Nicole Russo; Editor: Heather Moore Niver; Photo Researcher: Karen Huang